WHAT EVERY STUDENT SHOULD KNOW ABOUT CRITICAL READING

Ric Baker

Vivian Richardi Beitman

Delaware Technical Community College
Stanton, Delaware

PEARSON

Boston   Columbus   Indianapolis   New York   San Francisco   Upper Saddle River
Amsterdam   Cape Town   Dubai   London   Madrid   Milan   Munich   Paris   Montreal   Toronto
Delhi   Mexico City   São Paulo   Sydney   Hong Kong   Seoul   Singapore   Taipei   Tokyo

Executive Editor: Nancy Blaine
Director of Marketing: Megan Galvin-Fak
Editorial Assistant: Shannon Kobran
Senior Supplements Editor: Donna Campion
Project Coordination, Text Design, and Electronic Page Makeup: Grapevine Publishing
    Services, Inc.
Cover Designer: Alison Barth Burgoyne
Senior Manufacturing Buyer: Roy Pickering
Printer and Binder: Offset Paperback Manufacturing/Laflin
Cover Printer: Offset Paperback Manufacturing/Laflin

Please visit us at www.pearsonhighered.com

1 2 3 4 5 6 7 8 9 10   RRD   13 12 11

ISBN 13: 978-0-205-86992-3
ISBN 10:   0-205-86992-0

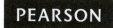

www.pearsonhighered.com

CONTENTS

PREFACE

Do you know how "critical reading" differs from "reading"? Or how "critical thinking" differs from "thinking"? This book will explain how to approach a variety of reading situations with a critical eye. The goal of critical thinking is to think systematically and rationally so that you can make better decisions and form beliefs that are more likely to be true. You will learn how to apply critical thinking skills to a text in order to decide whether it makes a good argument and if you should believe it. As you might suspect, thinking critically about a text requires hard work, but the benefits are tremendous. We will walk you through the steps to critical reading so that you are not overwhelmed by the process.

Chapter 1 provides you with an overview of the skills and attitudes involved with critical reading and thinking. You will learn about biases and obstacles to help you understand how difficult it is for some people to approach a text critically.

Chapter 2 stresses comprehension skills and reading strategies. Specifically, you will read about surveying, predicting, annotating, and learning new vocabulary.

Chapter 3 elaborates on the skills required to delve more deeply into a text. You will work on identifying the topic, determining the main idea, and recognizing details.

Chapter 4 is about making inferences, in particular about the author's purpose, audience, word connotations, and tone. You will realize that what an author *doesn't* say can be just as important and revealing as what the author *does* say.

Chapter 5 covers evaluation; specifically, you will learn how to recognize and judge arguments. Much of the focus is on evidence—both recognizing it and evaluating it. You will learn about evaluating sources as you determine whether or not an argument is believable and convincing. We will also examine two types of logic: inductive reasoning and deductive reasoning.

Chapter 6 introduces the skill of self-monitoring and how you can scrutinize worldviews and biases (your own as well as the author's).

Chapter 7, the last chapter, provides you with a review of the skills and traits inherent to critical readers and explains how you can use them throughout the rest of your life.

Each chapter has instructions "For Further Study" to give you some practice with critical reading. Most of the practices can be done on your own or with a classmate. These activities are designed to give you practical experience working with the skills, as well as food for thought. You will also find the "Learning More" feature at the end of every chapter. These questions get you thinking more intensely about the topics covered in the chapter and encourage you to research compelling ideas. All of the chapters contain relevant, accessible examples that help to illustrate new ideas. Finally, the chapters include visuals and bulleted lists to make concepts easier to comprehend and remember.

We hope that you will learn a great deal from this concise yet thorough overview of what it means to be a critical reader.

1

WHAT IS CRITICAL READING AND WHY IS IT IMPORTANT?

Critical reading is thinking critically about what you are reading. It means thinking carefully about a text in order to determine if the text is credible and believable, to decide if it presents a good argument or makes a good case, and to avoid being taken in by emotional manipulation and rhetorical tricks. Being a *critical reader* will carry over into all areas of your life, actually making you a better thinker.

To learn how to read critically, you have to know something about how to think critically, because critical reading means thinking critically about texts. *Critical thinking* is a reflective, rational process you can use to make good decisions or to form beliefs that are more likely to be true. Before you learn more about critical reading and thinking, though, let's explore why learning to read and think critically is so important.

Benefits of critical reading and thinking

Critical reading and critical thinking have some clear benefits. First, being able to read critically helps you do better in school. You will understand your homework better, you will be able to more effectively read your assignments, and you will get more out of them. In class, you will feel like you have a better grasp of the discussions and lessons, and you will be able to contribute to discussions. For these reasons, you will do better on tests, papers, and graded assignments, and you will get higher grades.

Getting good grades, of course, is the key to landing a job in the field of your choice after you graduate. On average, your happiness in life is directly related to how content you are in your job (second only to whom you choose for a mate). Critical reading involves critical thinking, and of course critical thinking applies to more than just reading texts. In fact, critical thinking is integral to most careers. Managers use critical thinking to determine what parts of their business strategy are working and what parts are not. When doctors and nurses try to figure out what is making a patient sick, they have to avoid preconceptions, consider all the evidence, and think carefully to arrive at the best diagnosis. Police officers need to avoid jumping to conclusions about who is guilty during an investigation, and they need to consider all the evidence in an unbiased manner, following where it leads. In fact, you will be more successful at any job that involves coming to conclusions or solving problems if you can read and think critically.

Critical readers and thinkers also handle problems in their daily lives more effectively. They tend to be more resilient and can handle stress better. They have lots of strategies and resources they can fall back on to get through life's challenges. On the other hand, people who can't read and think critically have more problems dealing with daily issues, and they don't handle stress as well.

Critical reading and thinking can also keep you from being deceived. People who don't know how to read and think effectively spend their money on medicines or procedures that don't work, such as magic crystals to cure cancer. They fall for scams on the Internet and sometimes get defrauded out of large sums of cash. They waste their money on fortunetellers and psychic hotlines instead of working to determine their own futures. They get scammed into signing unfavorable, complex mortgage contracts. Learning to read and think critically will help you avoid these pitfalls while being able to take advantage of the benefits.

FOR FURTHER STUDY

1. Brainstorm some ideas about what other benefits you might derive from becoming a better reader and thinker.
2. Research some actual cases in which people failed to read or think critically. What specific problems resulted?

Learning to read and think critically

To think critically about what you are reading, in other words, to read critically, you need to develop certain skills. You need to learn to:

- **Comprehend** the basic meaning of a text or speech, including previewing the text to learn what you will be reading about and to define difficult vocabulary.
- **Interpret** information, to make it clearer, including identifying the main ideas and pertinent details of a reading, as well as clarifying language that is vague or unclear.
- **Infer** conclusions from evidence, including identifying an author's audience, purpose, and tone.
- **Analyze** information, including recognizing an author's arguments and identifying the logic and evidence in the arguments.
- **Evaluate** an argument to determine if it is rightfully persuasive.
- **Monitor** your own thinking to avoid personal bias and to recognize bias in authors.

While all of these skills are crucial, the last skill in the list—self-monitoring—is especially important in critical reading and thinking. Our own biases and assumptions about the world will often lead us astray and cause us to make bad judgments or believe things that aren't true. Because every human being is prone to bias, if you want to learn to read and think critically, you need to work to develop certain attitudes that will help you avoid bias. Strive to be:

- **Curious.** Always seek to learn more about unfamiliar subjects.
- **Humble.** Avoid believing that you know everything, and accept that even if you're sure you're right, it's possible that you could be wrong.
- **Skeptical.** Don't believe a statement just because it has been printed in a book, newspaper, magazine, or on the Internet. Don't believe things just because people tell you they are true. Investigate for yourself, and only commit to believing something when you have good evidence that it's true.
- **Open-minded and flexible.** Always be open to new ideas and experiences, and be willing to change your viewpoint if new evidence comes along.
- **Fair-minded.** Don't give special consideration to an argument or claim just because you already agree with it or wish it were true. Make an effort to look for good points in arguments and claims you disagree with. Make sure that information—whether you are conveying it or receiving it—is accurate (meaning it is correct), clear (meaning it is not vague or ambiguous), complete

(meaning all necessary information is included), fair (meaning it is free from bias), relevant (meaning it applies to the situation), and significant (meaning it is important).

- **Persistent.** Don't give up! You'd be surprised what you can accomplish if you keep trying. In fact, persistence counts more in achieving your goals than talent, skill, or luck.

FOR FURTHER THOUGHT

1. Think of some other ways that you could use the skills of a critical thinker besides reading texts. What other things besides a piece of writing could you analyze or infer conclusions about, for example?
2. Do you already possess some of the attitudes of a critical thinker? Is so, which ones? Do you need to develop some of the attitudes mentioned? For example, do you need to work on your fair-mindedness? What are some specific ways you could develop the right attitudes?

Identifying your own biases and obstacles to critical reading and thinking

As a critical reader and thinker, not only will you develop certain skills and attitudes, but you will also have to be on the lookout for biases and obstacles that can get in the way of your ability to read and think critically. Everyone is biased, but the trick is to try to account for your own bias and to do your best not to let it affect you. For example, everyone wants to fit in, and so it becomes very difficult to go against the beliefs of your peers or community. If everyone in your community eats meat, for instance, it might be difficult to become a vegetarian. Critical readers and thinkers have to guard against *conformity*.

People also tend to favor their own viewpoints and to look for evidence to prove those viewpoints. This is called *confirmation bias*, because we tend to seek to confirm what we already believe, rather than challenge it. For example, if you believe that all pit bulls are vicious dogs, you will pay special attention to every news story involving a pit bull attack. However, you will overlook news stories involving other breeds biting people, and you will forget about all the very sweet pit bulls you have met. This is your brain's way of protecting the beliefs you already hold. Critical readers and thinkers are aware of confirmation bias and strive to avoid it. In fact, as a general rule, if you want to test if something you believe is true, look for evidence that it is false. Only if you fail to find any, after trying your hardest, can you feel confident in your belief.

Closely related to confirmation bias is *rationalization*. Rationalization is basically making excuses. You rationalize when you decide you want to do something (or not do something), and then look for reasons why it is acceptable. For example, if you want to download music illegally, so that you don't have to pay, your real reason for wanting to download the music is monetary—you'd rather keep the money to spend on something else while still getting the music—but you tell yourself that it is acceptable because if you didn't illegally download the song, you would never have bought it anyway, therefore the music company isn't really losing money. Of course this is simply an excuse. Perhaps these biases and obstacles sound familiar to you. We all rationalize. It is part of being human. But critical readers and thinkers learn to recognize when they are thinking in a biased way so that they can curb it.

The structure of this text

In the remainder of this text, you will work on developing the skills of a critical reader and thinker. In a sequential fashion, you will learn to comprehend a text by surveying it and predicting what you will find in it. You will learn to interpret what is significant in a text by identifying its topic, its main idea, and its relevant details. You'll learn to infer the audience, purpose, and tone of a reading. You'll learn to analyze any arguments the text makes and to evaluate whether the evidence and logic is sound. And finally, you will learn to identify bias in yourself and in the texts you're reading. While you are learning these skills, remember the attitudes of a critical reader and thinker; keep them in mind and apply them as you read texts and consider arguments. In this way you will gain a brief but comprehensive overview of what it means to read and think critically.

Learning More

1. There are more biases and obstacles to critical reading and thinking than just the three we've covered so far. Investigate biases further (possibly by doing a web search for "cognitive bias") and list three more biases. Try to pick biases you have come across in your own experience.

2. Using the Internet or your library, do a more comprehensive study of critical thinking. Write a one- to two-page essay wherein you define critical thinking in your own words. Try to find information that you didn't learn in this chapter.

3. Identify the class you currently struggle with the most. How do you feel learning to read critically could help you do better in that class? Be specific.

2

READING STRATEGIES: SURVEYING, PREDICTING, ANNOTATING, AND LEARNING NEW VOCABULARY

In the first chapter you learned that, as a critical reader and thinker, you can develop skills and attitudes to help you come to better decisions and to form beliefs that are more likely to be true. It is easier to acquire and remember new information when you are actively engaged with the text. Critical reading takes some hard work, but the payoff makes it worthwhile: a mastery of what you have read. As you think critically about what you read, you will use the following reading strategies to aid comprehension (one of the skills of a critical thinker): surveying, predicting, annotating, and learning new vocabulary.

Surveying

Surveying, also known as *previewing*, enables you to get an overview of a reading selection. Through surveying, you get the gist of the passage. In addition, surveying helps to awaken your curiosity (one of the attitudes of a critical thinker). Another advantage is that surveying activates your *prior knowledge*, the information you already know through personal experience and learning. Finally, if you take a few minutes to survey prior to reading the selection, you might be able to identify the topic, since it often appears in the title or is mentioned several times throughout the reading. In chapter 3, you will learn how knowing the topic can help you to figure out the main idea; so the topic is, indeed, important to comprehension.

Especially in textbooks, authors use visual cues to point readers in the direction of the main concepts. As you survey, take notice of items the author chooses to put in bold, italics, larger fonts, or different colors. Other visual cues you should recognize are boxes, highlighted text, and bulleted or numbered lists. Finally, take special note of any graphics—visual cues provided by the author, such as tables, illustrations, diagrams, and charts. In addition to these visual cues, textbook authors often include textual features to aid in comprehension. Before reading the entire chapter, read through these textual features:

- **Biographical notes**: In fields such as literature and philosophy, the author may give you a biography of a significant person to help you understand how that person's contributions influenced the events you will be reading about.
- **Chapter objectives**: Objectives are the goals of the chapter, so reading through these (typically on the first page of the chapter) will give focus to your study.
- **End-of-chapter questions**: These questions reveal what the author believes are the most important points for tests and quizzes. If you read these questions ahead of time, then, as you read the chapter (after you survey), you can answer them.
- **Historical notes**: Historical notes include pertinent information regarding a country, event, or historical era.
- **Introduction**: If the author provides you with an introduction to the chapter, read it; if not, then simply read the first paragraph or two.
- **Subheadings**: Subheadings, either set in bold or italics, and larger than the rest of the text (though smaller than the title and major headings), will provide you with each section's subtopic.
- **Summaries**: If the author provides you with a summary, be sure to read it, as it will sum up the primary ideas covered in the chapter; if there is not a formal summary, then read the last few paragraphs.
- **Text boxes**: Important supplemental information stands out in text boxes throughout the chapter; sometimes these boxes are graphically enhanced.
- **Title**: In textbooks, the title is frequently the topic or subject of the section. Knowing the topic helps comprehension greatly.

As you survey, you should come up with questions you expect will be answered once you have read the entire passage. Form questions about any items in bold, italics, and larger fonts. For example, say your history textbook has a subheading "Suffrage Movement." Quite easily and quickly, you could come up with several thought-provoking questions: What started the suffrage movement? When did it occur? Who were some important Americans involved in the suffrage movement? How did women's suffrage later influence African Americans who wanted the right to vote? By asking questions while you survey, you give yourself something to look for and focus on when you read the chapter.

FOR FURTHER STUDY

1. Survey a chapter from one of your college textbooks. Which visual cues are the most helpful, in your opinion?
2. Using the same chapter, write a list of three questions you think will be answered in the text. Then, read the chapter and see if you do, in fact, learn answers to those questions.
3. Write a short paragraph that explains how surveying a reading passage can awaken in you at least two of the attitudes of a critical thinker: intellectual humility and curiosity.

Predicting

In addition to surveying, another useful reading strategy for you to learn is *predicting*—an active mental process that requires you to make guesses about what might happen next in the passage. Begin with the questions you posed while you surveyed the text, and make predictions about what some of the answers will be. You can also make predictions about how what you are reading might relate to what you are learning in class.

Prediction is a helpful reading and studying strategy. When you predict, you have to pay attention to what you are reading in order to make connections. One advantage of predicting is that it enables you to see the information as a whole, instead of separate parts. Through predicting, you can see how the topic and subtopics relate to one another. One of the skills of a critical thinker is *analysis*—

breaking down an idea into its component parts in order to understand the whole more fully. Predicting can shed new light on your analysis of an argument or text.

FOR FURTHER STUDY

1. Pick an article or chapter you need to read for a college class. Write down at least three predictions before you read the material. At the end of the reading, note whether each prediction was correct or not.
2. Think about a movie or play you saw recently. Were you able to make predictions early on in the show? Were you right? Did the act of making predictions keep you more involved in the storyline or not? Explain.

Annotating

Another essential reading strategy to learn is annotating. *Annotating* is the strategy of marking the crucial elements of the text. If you make it a point to read with a pencil in hand, you will greatly improve your understanding of the reading. Annotating is an active reading strategy that helps you to stay focused and engaged with the text.

As you become more proficient at annotating, you may develop your own personal style. In the meantime, here are some ideas to get you started:

1. Underline the topic of the reading (often stated in the title or in a word or short phrase mentioned throughout the reading).
2. Label important or surprising information with an asterisk or exclamation point.
3. Put a question mark next to any confusing parts.
4. Formulate your own questions about the text and write them in the margin.
5. Look up new vocabulary words and write each definition above the word or in the margin.
6. Write down your predictions as you read.

7. If the author makes statements that you strongly agree or disagree with, mark them down.

Chances are, at some point in your academic career you learned about main ideas, details, transitions, and emotive words. In later chapters, we will review these concepts. You will also want to mark them in a reading passage:

1. Double-underline or highlight the stated main idea.
2. If the main idea is implied (hinted at or suggested), then paraphrase it in the margin.
3. Label supporting details.
4. Circle transitions that show how the text is organized and shifts in the author's train of thought.
5. Circle emotive words that suggest something the author feels strongly about.

If reading tends to make you sleepy, then annotating will keep you more alert; making decisions about what to mark keeps your brain fully engaged and attentive. Yet another advantage of annotating is that your marks become study notes if you are to be tested on the material.

Learning new vocabulary

The last strategy to cover in this chapter is developing your vocabulary. Think for a moment about why you should bother to learn new vocabulary words. You probably came up with some or all of these reasons: A strong word base makes reading easier. A good grasp of language makes you a better writer. A command of vocabulary makes you more interesting and persuasive in discussions. People who read a lot tend to have strong vocabularies. Even so, there are hundreds of thousands of words in the English language; as you read you are bound to encounter some that need to be defined. Improving your vocabulary will make your college reading load more manageable, and will also make reading more enjoyable for the rest of your life.

In this chapter, you will learn how to use context clues, word parts, and dictionaries, and you will also learn how to study vocabulary. First, however, see if you can define the following words without the use of a dictionary: (1) *onomatopoeia* (2) *recluse* (3) *prolific* (4) *prevalent*. If you aren't sure of the definitions, don't worry—you will see them again in a practice exercise on context clues later in the chapter.

Context clues

A *context clue* is another word or piece of information surrounding an unfamiliar word that gives hints about the word's meaning. While a dictionary gives you the most accurate definition of a word, it can be time-consuming and not always practical to get out a dictionary or go online to look up a word. Context clues allow you to get the general sense of the word's meaning. The four most common types of context clues are definitions, synonyms, antonyms, and examples.

Definition—A definition context clue can be most obvious and helpful, as this "clue" is the actual definition of the new word. Authors may put the definition close to the word in question, and it may be set off by punctuation, such as dashes or commas. In textbooks, the new word might be set in bold or italics, and the definition may directly follow it. Sometimes authors will use signal words such as *is, means,* or *is defined as* to bring your attention to the definition. An example of a definition context clue is in the following sentence:

> One of the three parts of the psyche, the **id,** is supposedly the unconscious and childlike source of instinctive desires, according to Sigmund Freud's psychoanalytic theory.

Synonym—A synonym is a word that means the same or nearly the same as the unfamiliar word. The synonym may be a word that is more common to the reader, so it will shed light on the brand-new word. Authors may use punctuation such as commas or a signal word such as *or* to signal a synonym. The following sentence contains a synonym context clue:

> Julie did not appreciate Henry's **acerbic** sense of humor on their first date; she thought his sharp jokes were directed at her.

The word "sharp" is the synonym for the less familiar "acerbic."

Antonym—An antonym is a word of opposite meaning. In this case, the opposite of a word that is unfamiliar to the reader. When the author shows what a new word does *not* mean by identifying its antonym, the reader can figure out its meaning. Signal words include contrast words such as *in contrast, unlike, but, rather,* and *opposed to.* The following sentence contains an antonym:

> Stan had a bad habit of making **inane** comments in class in order to get attention, but his classmates who made intelligent comments received far more positive feedback.

The signal word "but" tells you that "inane" and "intelligent" are antonyms, so you can understand that "inane" means "silly" or "unintelligent."

Example—An example is a situation, person, instance, or item that serves as a case or illustration of the vocabulary word. Authors might use these signal words: *for example, for instance, such as,* and *like.* The following sentence gives examples of items that are "requisite" for college students:

> When you go to college, do not forget to budget for **requisite** supplies such as pens, pencils, paper, printer ink, notebooks, and folders.

In this sentence, the items "pens, pencils..." represent indispensable school supplies, so you conclude that "requisite" means "necessary" or "essential."

Figuring out the meanings of words using context clues takes practice. In addition, you might only get a general sense of the definition and may still want to consult a dictionary. Remember to annotate as you read and record any new definitions. Finally, as with all new words, you need to use them frequently in conversation and in writing to make them a part of your working vocabulary (the words you are most comfortable using on a daily basis).

Practice

Directions: Read the following sentences. Words that may be unfamiliar to you are set in bold. Underline the context clue used for

each new word. In the space provided for you, try to write the definition in your own words (do not consult a dictionary yet), and
write down which type of context clue was used (definition, synonym, antonym, or example). Each will be used only once. Finally,
refer to a dictionary to see if the context clue led you to a close
approximation of the dictionary definition.

1. **Onomatopoeia,** a word you are sure to come across in your
   poetry classes, means to label something by the sound that it
   makes or resembles (like "hiss").
   Definition of onomatopoeia: _____
   Type of context clue used: _____

2. Emily Dickinson, a **recluse,** led a life that was in sharp contrast to that of social extroverts, and this reclusive lifestyle
   resulted in her writing almost 2,000 poems.
   Definition of recluse: _____
   Type of context clue used: _____

3. After meeting with commercial success, many poets become
   prolific in their art; for example, both Robert Frost and W. B.
   Yeats wrote a significant number of poems and plays.
   Definition of prolific: _____
   Type of context clue used: _____

4. Perhaps part of the reason why poetry is so **prevalent** or wide-
   spread throughout the world is due to our need as humans to
   express ourselves and make connections with others.
   Definition of prevalent: _____
   Type of context clue used: _____

Word parts

In addition to using context clues to improve your vocabulary, you
can work on recognizing root words, prefixes, and suffixes. The
most basic form of a word, the *root*, can be modified by adding
prefixes and suffixes. *Prefixes* are word parts put at the beginning
of a root word in order to make a new word. *Suffixes,* added to the
end of a root word to create a new word, are word parts that
change the original word's part of speech or tense.

Sometimes a combining vowel, *o*, joins the word parts to aid in pronunciation (such as in "cardiology" which combines *cardi* and *logy*):

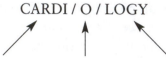

CARDI / O / LOGY

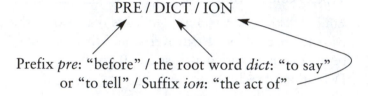

Root *cardi*: "heart" / Combining *o* / Suffix *log*: "study of"

In addition, a word can be formed by using more than one root word, prefix, or suffix, as in "prediction," which combines a prefix, root word, and suffix to mean "the act of telling before."

PRE / DICT / ION

Prefix *pre*: "before" / the root word *dict*: "to say"
or "to tell" / Suffix *ion*: "the act of"

Some words do not include a prefix or suffix, and sometimes groups of letters that spell a common prefix or suffix do not have the same meaning (such as *log*, meaning either "speech," "study of," or "words"). The lexicons of many fields, including the medical and legal professions, consist of words created by using word parts. Learning word parts enables you to build your vocabulary quickly.

FOR FURTHER STUDY

1. Go online and search for "word parts." Print out a list of root words, prefixes, and suffixes. Brainstorm a list of words you already know that contain those word parts. Finally, commit to memory some common root words, prefixes, and suffixes.

2. As you are reading your college textbooks, keep a list of new vocabulary words that contain root words, prefixes, and suffixes. Break up each word into its component parts, and label each with an arrow (as done with "cardiology" and "prediction" above). See if your understanding of word parts helps you to learn the new words.

Dictionaries

Both online and print dictionaries contain lists of words and their meanings organized alphabetically. A dictionary also provides valuable information, such as the correct spelling and pronunciation. Oftentimes, the dictionary entry contains several possible definitions, which are numbered; you need to know how the word is being used in context in order to select the correct definition. A dictionary includes the following features to provide a better understanding of each word:

- **Guidewords** are words at the top of each page of a print dictionary that indicate the range of words located on that page. For example, if you see "disguise" and "disturb" at the top of the page, then you know you could find the word "dismount" on that page.
- **Etymology** tells you about the origin and history of a word.
- **Syllabification** is provided by dots, dashes, or slashes to show how words break down into units or syllables.
- **Part of speech** is given through abbreviations; for example, noun (n.), verb, verb transitive (v., vt.), adjective (adj.), etc.
- **Spelling modifications** are often included to show what happens when a suffix is added to a word: for example, the plural of "guppy" is "guppies."

An online dictionary, such as www.m-w.com and www.dictionary .com, will include a sound file so that you can hear the correct pronunciation of a word. Once you know what the word means and how to say it properly, you should make it part of your working vocabulary by using it frequently.

FOR FURTHER STUDY

Look up the words in the exercise on context clues (*onomatopoeia, recluse, prolific,* and *prevalent*) in a print dictionary. Fill out a chart that includes the following information:

- Guidewords for each word listed at the top of the page
- Syllabification
- Part of speech
- Definition as it is being used in context of the practice exercise

How to study vocabulary

As with all concepts you will encounter during your years in college, you need to study and practice in order to master new words. Reading them once or twice or looking them up in a dictionary is probably not going to be enough for you to commit the definitions to your long-term memory. If you learn new words for a quiz or test but never use them in conversation and writing, you are likely to forget them. Remember, your goal is not merely to learn new words to pass the test; your goal is to boost your vocabulary so that you will be a more efficient reader, more interesting writer, and more proficient conversationalist! Use the study techniques below to improve your chances of memorizing vocabulary words.

> **Index cards**—If your middle school and high school teachers introduced you to this method, there is a good reason: It works. However, it only works if you actually take your index cards with you and practice them whenever you have a few minutes (when you are waiting for a bus or for class to begin, for instance). On the unlined side of the card, write the new word. Then, on the lined side, write the definition, part of speech, pronunciation, and the sentence in which you first encountered the word. Next, write an original sentence using the word correctly. Some words lend themselves well to drawings or pictures; include one if possible, especially if you are a visual learner.

Unlined side of index card:

Ubiquitous

Lined side of index card:

Definition: Omnipresent, pervasive, everywhere

Part of speech: Adjective—Pronunciation: \yü-ˈbi-kwə-təs\

First encountered word: My professor said in class, "The common cockroach is ubiquitous in many regions of the world."

Original sentence: Every September on campus, the ubiquitous college sweatshirt advertises the fact that the new students are excited to spend their money at the college bookstore.

As you study your index cards, say the word out loud. (Remember, you can go to an online dictionary such as www.m-w.com or www.dictionary.com and click on the pronunciation icon to hear it.) Test yourself to see if you remember the definition. When you are confident you have mastered a word, put that card in a pile of words to practice later. Then, you can focus on the pile of cards that you have not yet mastered. You should also mix up the order of the cards frequently—sometimes students will learn a list of vocabulary words in order and then have trouble if the words are presented in a different order on a quiz! In addition, have a friend quiz you to verify that you have, indeed, learned the new words.

Sticky notes—This method works especially well if you have a few words that are giving you trouble. Use a separate note for each word. Write the word and its definition on the front side of a note, and stick it in a spot where you will see it frequently. Then, put these notes on your bathroom mirror, your refrigerator, your car dashboard, and around the perimeter of your computer monitor—anywhere you will study the word several times throughout the day. When you need to recall the definition on a test or quiz, you will be able to "see" the note with the word and its definition in your mind.

Pretend to be the teacher—If you were the teacher, how would you get students to learn challenging vocabulary? You could create a PowerPoint presentation, complete with the word's pronunciation in a sound file. Perhaps you would make up a crossword puzzle or a quiz.

Study partner—Finally, you could meet up with a study partner and test each other.

None of these study techniques will take up too much of your time, yet each one will result in a better ability to remember your new vocabulary words.

The benefits of mastering new vocabulary cannot be overstated. You will see immediate improvements in your reading ability and your schoolwork. Long-term, you will gain the reputation of being a person who speaks and writes with a strong command of vocabulary.

Learning More

1. Reflect on your current reading habits and think about how you will incorporate what you learned in this chapter. Which reading strategy do you think you will find most helpful? Least helpful? Explain.
2. Some of the pointers given in this chapter pertain to reading textbooks in particular. How can you adapt what you learned to other types of reading (reading newspapers, reading for pleasure, reading contracts, personal documents, etc.)?
3. Explain how you can modify each of these strategies (surveying, predicting, annotating, and developing vocabulary) to help you comprehend visual media, such as a documentary film, a political debate, or a speech.

3

IDENTIFYING TOPIC, MAIN IDEA, AND DETAILS

In chapter 1, you learned about the importance of critical reading and thinking, and in chapter 2, you worked on some useful reading strategies. Now you will practice identifying the topic, main idea, and details.

While you probably have some understanding of these concepts from your academic career so far, if you are like most students, you might still struggle on occasion. Becoming proficient in identifying topic, main idea, and details will make a tremendous difference in your ability to read efficiently and confidently.

Identifying the topic

Identifying the topic of a selection helps lead you to other essential parts of the reading—the main idea, major details, and minor details—so it is important that you master this skill. Another word for topic is *subject*. The topic is typically stated in a word or short phrase.

As you learned in chapter 2, the topic of the reading selection often appears in the title or in a section heading. Subtopics will appear in subheadings.

The topic also tends to be repeated throughout the paragraph, chapter, or article. If you are annotating (perhaps by underlining or highlighting key terms), then you should notice if the same words or phrases keep appearing.

When identifying the topic, try to avoid the common mistake of picking a word or short phrase from the text that is either too broad or general, or too specific or detailed to accurately describe the topic. Pretend to be Goldilocks as you make your way through a passage: You don't want a topic that is "too big" or "too small"; you want the one that is "just right." For example, if your refrigerator broke down and you had to shop for a new one, you would not tell the salesperson that you needed an "appliance" because that would be too broad and general; "appliance" could easily mean dishwasher or stove. Nor would you say that you need a 22.9 cubic foot side-by-side refrigerator; that would be too specific and detailed. Instead, you would explain that you are shopping for a refrigerator, and you would then be directed to the appropriate location in the store to make your selection.

FOR FURTHER STUDY

1. Select one of your textbooks from another class and read a paragraph. Identify the "just right" topic. Then, determine what word or phrase might be mistaken for the topic but is too broad/general, and what word or phrase is too specific/detailed.
2. Write two to three paragraphs about how some topics are sure to arouse the attitudes of a critical thinker in you. Be specific. (For example, the topic "psychic ability" might make some readers immediately feel skeptical.) What topics make you feel open-minded, intellectually humble, and so on?

Identifying details

Authors use *details* to support, develop, and elaborate upon the topic, so noticing details will get you closer to your goal of identifying the main idea of a passage. Details are often the answers to the questions *who, what, where, when, why,* and *how,* referred to as "reporter's questions." Authors frequently organize their details through the use of *patterns of organization,* also known as *thought patterns,* which help to arrange the information in a logical manner. Common patterns of organization include cause and effect, chronological order, classification, comparison/contrast, definition, example, and listing. Also, authors may use a mixed pattern when they need to employ two or more patterns of organization to best arrange the evidence. Patterns of organization often make use of *transitions*—words that suggest organization as well as the author's train of thought. Transitions can point you in the direction of details, so if you are annotating the passage, you should circle transition words that lead you to important details. The following chart lists common transitions by patterns of organization:

Patterns of Organization	Description	Transition words
Cause and Effect	Authors choose this pattern to explain the causes (reasons) for an effect (consequence, outcome, event). Sometimes an author will focus on a single cause that results in several effects, or the author will look at many causes that lead to one effect.	causes, reasons, effects results, happens, because, since, source, consequence, outcome, leads to
Chronological	Chronological order (also known as time order) is used to organize narratives (stories) or processes (how to do something or how something works). Biographies and historical events often depend on chronological order.	first, second, finally, soon, after, next, later, at the same time, since, when, during, throughout, last month, ten years ago, upcoming
Classification	Classification is used to categorize, classify, or order assorted topics and to show why they belong in a particular class. Authors will use classification to explain the traits that topics in a certain class have in common.	categorize, classify, characteristics, traits, types, classes, qualities

Patterns of Organization	Description	Transition words
Comparison and Contrast	Authors use comparison and/or contrast to show how two or more items are similar and/or different.	Compare: to compare, similar, as, same, both, in comparison Contrast: but, however, on the other hand, in contrast, unlike, differences
Definition	The definition pattern is used to give the meaning and characteristics of a new term; this is a common pattern in textbooks.	means, is, defined as, termed
Example	Authors use the example pattern when they need to give ample evidence and details that develop or prove a thesis.	for example, in this case, to illustrate, such as, some, few, many, one reason, another point, to explain
Listing	With the listing pattern, authors can provide several ideas (of equal level of importance) that work together to support the main idea.	also, in addition, another, moreover, furthermore, besides
Mixed	Authors sometimes combine two or more patterns of development to explain their main idea effectively.	variety of transitions

You should understand, however, that authors use whatever transitions seem natural to them as they are getting a point across to their readers. This could cause a passage that is primarily one pattern of organization to contain some transitions that are more common to other patterns. In the following paragraph, which uses the cause and effect pattern, transitions are underlined. You will recognize cause and effect transitions as well as ones that are more typically found in other patterns:

> What <u>led to</u> the demise of the dinosaurs? Most groups of dinosaurs (with the exception of certain <u>types</u> of birds) became extinct approximately 65 million <u>years ago</u>. <u>Several reasons</u> contributed to the <u>effect</u> known as the Cretaceous-Paleogene extinction event. <u>One cause</u> involved changes in temperature <u>and</u> atmosphere <u>because</u> a decrease in volcanic activity cooled the air <u>and</u> altered levels of carbon dioxide <u>and</u> oxygen. Lowered oxygen levels posed serious problems for those dinosaurs with enormous bodies that needed huge amounts of oxygen to function efficiently. <u>Another reason</u> was <u>due to</u> a meteorite strike in the Yucatan Peninsula, Mexico, that greatly <u>affected</u> the atmospheric temperatures. <u>Since</u> temperature changes <u>also</u> <u>affected</u> plants <u>such as</u> angiosperms and gymnosperms, the dinosaurs who depended on these as food sources could not survive <u>when</u> they were no longer thriving in the ecosystem.

Notice that, of course, not all of the transitions in the paragraph about dinosaurs point to cause and effect. *Such as* is a transition frequently used in the example pattern, and *when* is a chronological transition. However, the majority of the transitions are common to the cause and effect pattern, and, most important, the topic of the paragraph is about what led to dinosaur extinction. In other words, what were the *causes* of dinosaur extinction.

There are two kinds of details: major details and minor details, and they vary in their degree of specificity. *Major details* directly support the main idea, while *minor details* develop the major details or make the writing more interesting and memorable. While the major details are medium-specific, the minor details tend to be very specific. When you are figuring out the main idea, the major details are more important and crucial. Do not get too hung up on the tiniest of minor details; instead, focus your attention on the major details. The next example paragraph, using chronological order, contains a lot of details. You would be overwhelmed if you were expected to remember each and every detail. Instead, focus on the major details, which are underlined, to get a thorough understanding of the topic.

Planning a successful party takes a lot of work ahead of time to ensure that even the hosts enjoy themselves. <u>First, you need to come up with a guest list and the approximate number of people you expect will attend.</u> Once you know how many guests you are dealing with, <u>you can then decide where to have it.</u> If you decide to have it at home, be reasonable: Most houses cannot accommodate 150+ guests, but if you are having a much smaller party, then your own home is the most economical choice. If you are having a big party, then you will need to contact restaurants, banquet halls, and community centers to check availability for the date of your party. <u>Soon after, you should arrange for music, entertainment, food, and drinks.</u> If you are having outside vendors provide services or products (such as music or flowers), then make sure you get a signed contract. <u>If you haven't done so already, during this time you should enlist some reliable friends and family members to help you make arrangements. When you plan for food and drinks, assume that most guests will eat two helpings of side dishes and drink up to four beverages.</u> Include plenty of nonalcoholic drinks such as water, soft drinks, iced tea, and lemonade, and make sure you have designated drivers who are willing to drive people home if necessary. <u>Purchase paper products, decorations, party favors, and serving trays and dishes.</u> Throughout the planning of the event, <u>keep to-do lists handy</u> so that you do not forget any important details. Finally, let all of the planning pay off so that you can have a fantastic time!

Minor details can help make the paragraph more interesting and persuasive, but you do not need to remember every last little minor detail. For instance, you do not have to remember the author's point about getting lemonade—that is a minor detail—but you should fully grasp that you need to arrange for drinks, including nonalcoholic ones.

Remember, authors carefully select major and minor details that develop their main idea. By identifying the details, you can examine how they add up to give you the overall impression that the author wants to convey about the topic.

FOR FURTHER STUDY

1. Select one of your textbooks from another class and read a paragraph. Annotate the paragraph, paying particular attention to the transitions that signal details. Label each detail either "major" or "minor."
2. Read an article or a chapter that is assigned for another class. Determine which pattern of organization the author used to arrange the details.
3. Write a sample paragraph that uses a mixed pattern of organization (pick two to combine).

Identifying the main idea

The strategies you have learned so far in this book (surveying, predicting, annotating, developing vocabulary, finding the topic, and locating details), have led you to this point: identifying the author's main idea. The *main idea* is the most important idea in a passage, and recognizing the main idea is crucial to critical reading. Typically, the main idea is the most general idea in a reading. The main idea might also be referred to as the author's claim about the topic. A *claim* is a statement that is open to challenge or disagreement. In addition, the main idea is known as the *controlling idea*. In a paragraph, if the main idea is stated directly, it is called a *topic sentence*. In a longer piece of writing (usually two or more paragraphs), the main idea is referred to as a *thesis* or *thesis statement*.

If you can point to a single sentence in a paragraph or essay that functions as the main idea, it is a *stated main idea* (again, if it is in a paragraph, it will be called a topic sentence; if it is in a longer passage, it will be called a thesis). Topic sentences are frequently at the beginning and/or end of the paragraph, but they can also appear anywhere in a paragraph; in a longer passage. A stated thesis statement frequently appears at the end of the first or last paragraph, but, like a topic sentence, it can be anywhere. Not all main ideas are stated, however. In contrast to a stated main idea, an *implied main idea* is not written out in one clear, direct sentence. When the main idea is implied, the reader must figure out the main idea by carefully examining details and word choices to identify the author's opinion or controlling idea. If you read a paragraph or a longer essay with an implied main idea, then it is an excellent idea to annotate by paraphrasing the implied main idea in the margin.

The sample paragraph below (using the example pattern of development) contains a stated main idea (underlined):

> <u>Physical and emotional stressors can affect your ability to think critically.</u> For example, when you are tired or anxious, then you are less likely to look carefully at all sides of an issue. Students who are exhausted from taking eighteen credits a semester have reported that they believe everything they read because they simply don't have the time or energy to research other perspectives. As another example, people who are going through stressors, such as divorce or job loss claim that they have a hard time evaluating an argument for weaknesses and bias. In one instance, a classmate whose mother died recently ended up making terrible financial decisions because he trusted a shady investor, and he lost most of his inheritance. If you are going through a tough time physically or emotionally, it helps to delay making important decisions until you feel better and can think more critically.

The next paragraph has an implied main idea:

> In general, college students fall into one of two groups: traditional and nontraditional. Traditional college students attend college directly after graduating from high school. They are typically in their late teens when they start college and attain their degree in their early twenties. While many of them have part-time jobs, their work obligations tend not to interfere too much with their academics. Other qualities the traditional students share include an enthusiasm for extracurricular college activities and a tendency to spend most of their free time with their peers (often on the college campus). The second group, made up of nontraditional students, can also

be called "returning adult students." The members of the nontraditional group pursued other endeavors before they decided to go to college, so they are older than the traditional students. Many of them worked, spent years in the military, or raised children. Traits these nontraditional students share with each other include the ability to juggle their assorted responsibilities and the desire to make big changes in their lives through education. In a college classroom, it is not unusual to see both types of college students collaborating with each other on projects.

You should put the main idea in a single sentence in your own words and write it in the margin of your book. In the above paragraph, the author would want you to remember something like this: *The two types of college students are traditional and nontraditional students. Traditional students are younger and tend to spend a lot of time with peers on campus, whereas nontraditional students did other things after getting out of high school and may have additional work and family obligations beyond the classroom.*

Oftentimes you will need to reread a passage several times in order to identify the main idea. As you read, and reread, you should carefully examine the topic and the details. You want to figure out what it is that the author is claiming or stating about the topic. Ask yourself, What is the author's opinion about the topic? As you know, various authors might write about the exact same topic but have different opinions about it, and therefore, they will express different main ideas. Here is an example:

Topic: *Politicians in America*
Author 1: Politicians are self-centered, self-righteous people who pretend to care about issues in order to get elected.
Author 2: Politicians are idealist dreamers who have the best interests of Americans at heart but who have to deal with the complicated world of lobbyists and political pundits.
Author 3: Politicians may start out with good intentions, but the two-party system that plagues Washington, D.C. ruins them.
Author 4: Politicians are terribly out of touch with the real concerns of the American people.

Similar to how some transitions point to details, other transitions may point directly to the main ideas. Look for transitions that signal *emphasis or level of importance* (such as *above all*), as well as any transitions that indicate a *conclusion* (such as *in conclusion*). The following chart lists transitions directing you to the main idea:

Transitions that Signal Main Ideas	
Emphasis, Level of Importance	above all, in fact, without a doubt
Conclusion	in conclusion, in summary, therefore, thus, consequently

In the paragraph below, which uses the listing pattern of organization, the author used a transition showing emphasis/level of importance to signal the main idea (underlined):

> Most Americans are familiar with pasta dishes that originated in Italy. Spaghetti and lasagna are staples at the dinner table. In addition, American diners often enjoy linguini, especially with seafood. Another Italian favorite is ravioli, which is typically filled with meat or cheese. Besides finding ravioli on the menu, you could order tortellini, another pasta variety that is filled with additional ingredients. Moreover, Americans appreciate other delicious dishes such as gnocchi and fettuccine. Children all over the world tend to prefer macaroni and cheese above all the other Italian choices. <u>Without a doubt, whether you are in America or Italy, you are sure to find a huge variety of pasta on the menu since Italian favorites have been embraced by Americans.</u>

Authors vary widely in the number and type of transitions they use. You may come across details and main ideas that are not introduced by any transitions at all. Careful reading and annotating should reveal the main idea, even if the author does not provide you with an obvious transition, such as *therefore*.

Other words you should observe and annotate are emotive words. *Emotive words* are words that express opinion, judgment, or emotion. Authors use emotive words when they experience strong feelings about the topic, so noticing these words will provide insight into the author's main idea. The following list gives examples of typical emotive words:

Aesthetic	attractive, wonderful, unappealing, ugly
Judgment	advantages, disadvantages, pros, cons, bad, good
Recommendation	can, should, must, ought to
Superlative	best, worst, least, most

Remember that the main idea expresses the author's opinion regarding the topic, so if the author uses an emotive word (and emotive words express opinions), you should pay attention and ask yourself how the emotive word contributes to the overall impression the author wants to convey. The next paragraph uses a comparison and contrast pattern and contains several emotive words (underlined):

Two classic figures in American literature, Ernest Hemingway and F. Scott Fitzgerald, share some striking similarities, but, like most creative people, they were ultimately unique. Both are considered masters of early twentieth-century literature and even spent time together in Paris, where both men were influenced heavily by other artists and writers living in Europe in the 1920s. Similarly, they were considered members of the "Lost Generation" of artists who served in World War I, and both were alcoholics. In addition, the two writers had books made into films. Despite these similarities, there were some important differences. Best known for such moving novels as *The Sun Also Rises, A Farewell to Arms,* and *The Old Man and the Sea*, Hemingway worked as a journalist before writing full time. Fitzgerald, on the other hand, worked in advertising prior to turning to a writing career and wrote plays in addition to short stories and <u>touching</u> novels, such as *The Great Gatsby* and *Tender Is the Night*. Whereas Hemingway's writing centered on war and struggles against nature, Fitzgerald's works focused on material success and romantic relationships. While Hemingway died of a self-inflicted gunshot wound, Fitzgerald died from a heart attack brought on by <u>poor</u> health related to alcoholism and tuberculosis.

Given the use of emotive words such as "striking," "unique," and "touching," it would appear that the author is impressed with the literary accomplishments of Hemingway and Fitzgerald and finds their similarities and differences to be important. By carefully annotating emotive words, you will have greater insight into the opinion of the author.

After you have taken the time to read, annotate, reread, and closely examine the topic, details, and word choices, you should ask yourself some questions:

- What is the author's most important point?
- What is the author's opinion regarding the topic?
- What would the author want me to remember?
- If I had to tell a friend about this passage in one single sentence, what would I say?
- If I could only take away one piece of information from this passage, what would it be?

The answer to any one of these questions could be the main idea. Remember, if it is a stated main idea, then you will be able to double-underline or highlight a sentence within the passage. If it is an implied main idea, then you will need to put it in your own words in a single sentence. This, by the way, takes some practice! Try to be brief and clear. How would you explain it to a friend? If it helps, say it out loud first and then write it in the margin of the passage you are annotating.

To summarize this critical reading skill, you identify the main idea using the following steps:

1. Read and annotate.
2. Identify the topic in a word or short phrase.

3. Highlight any transitions or emotive words.
4. Examine details.
5. Think about the overall impression the author is sharing with readers. Ask yourself questions about what the author would want you to know and remember.
6. Reread the passage and see if the author has included a stated main idea anywhere within the selection. Double-underline or highlight a stated main idea.
7. If the main idea is not stated, then it is implied. In your own words, write the main idea in a single sentence, and put it in the margin.

FOR FURTHER STUDY

1. Annotate the sample paragraphs. Be sure to mark transitions and emotive words. If the paragraph has a stated main idea, double-underline or highlight it. If it has an implied main idea, paraphrase it in the margin.
2. Figuring out the main idea takes a lot of work. Write a paragraph explaining how the attitude of persistence helps as you try to identify the main idea of a long passage.

Being able to identify the topic, details, and main idea of a reading will help you tremendously as you endeavor to tackle your academic load. Even after you graduate from college, however, you will continue to use these strategies to understand what you read. While this book focuses on reading college material, be aware that you can use your ability to figure out topic, details, and main idea in a variety of situations. For example, if you are listening to a political speech, you should certainly listen carefully to identify the politician's main idea so that you can determine if you agree with it. As another example, in your future career, you are sure to receive memos, emails, and reports from colleagues and bosses, and you must utilize these same skills to examine the topic, details, and main idea of the correspondence so that you can do your job effectively. Knowing how to approach information, scrutinize it, and make decisions about what it conveys is a crucial critical thinking skill.

Learning More

1. In the previous paragraph, you read how you would use the skills covered in this chapter to interpret a political speech. Come up with an original example, and write a paragraph that gives a scenario describing how you might use these skills to approach information that is not in written format.

2. Write a short essay that describes an instance when you misunderstood information. What happened when you got the topic, details, and main idea wrong? How could you do better in the future?

4

MAKING INFERENCES AND RECOGNIZING AUTHOR'S PURPOSE, AUDIENCE, AND TONE

Making inferences means to take in information, think about the details and how they relate to what you already know, and then reach a logical conclusion. An inference is a guess, or rather, a reasonable guess. Critical readers are skilled at inference—arriving at a reasonable conclusion based on what is presented in the text. Authors *imply* (hint or suggest) ideas at times rather than state every idea directly. Another word for inference is *conclusion*. Drawing conclusions based on what is indirectly shared by an author is an important skill because it enables you to grasp more completely the author's entire message, both what is being said overtly and what is being implied.

As a critical reader, some of the most important things you will have to infer are an author's purpose, audience, word connotations, and tone. Learning how to read between the lines and figure out the author's likely purpose (goal for writing) helps you understand more about the author, and, consequently, more about the text itself. Examining the author's intended audience allows you to think about what characteristics those audience members have in common and how they might influence the text. In addition, words that have strong connotations create images in the readers' minds that help get the author's message across. Finally, detecting the author's tone (voice) assists you in gaining a better sense of the author's attitude and feeling about the subject.

Forming inferences

We make inferences every day. If you see a car on the side of the highway, you may infer that the driver had car trouble or some sort of emergency that caused him to pull over. To draw an accurate conclusion, you might need to ask some questions or do some research to find out exactly what happened. Isn't it possible that the driver had to pull over to take care of a small child? Couldn't the driver have stopped to verify directions or to take a nap? Sometimes your original inference needs to be adjusted as new evidence comes into play. The same is true as you draw conclusions while reading. You should strive to study as much information as possible so that you can arrive at a justifiable conclusion.

As children, many of you completed connect-the-dot pictures, in which you were given a handout with a partial outline of a shape, such as a robot or dolphin, and you had to use a crayon to connect the numbered dots that would finish forming the shape. Think of drawing inferences as connecting the dots. An author gives you the basic form—the dots—and it is up to you to make the logical connections between them.

As you work on filling in any information that the author does not state directly, you should annotate. Annotating inferences in the margin of the text helps you keep track of your tentative conclusions; as you read further, your initial inferences might change. The following directions explain how to make inferences:

1. **Make sure you understand the material.** First check your comprehension of the author's explicitly stated message by identifying the topic, asking questions, examining details, and defining vocabulary words.
2. **Clarify any difficult passages.** Annotate the reading, summarize the main idea and major details in your own words, or create a visual if needed.
3. **Notice subtleties.** Pay attention to what is being implied or hinted at by the author.
4. **Refer to the text repeatedly.** Continue to go back to the text over and over again to make sure your inferences are on track. Do not let your own experiences or biases lead you in a direction that is not supported by the text.

5. **Do additional reading.** Sometimes you cannot make a logical inference without doing some further reading and research. Recognize when you need to read more in order to connect the dots.

FOR FURTHER STUDY

1. Read a crime novel or a mystery to practice making inferences. Try to figure out who the perpetrator is before the author reveals it.
2. Brainstorm a list of situations in the past week in which you made inferences. How did you know whether or not you were drawing logical conclusions? Did you ever have to adjust your initial inference based on new information?

Inferring an author's audience

As you work on drawing logical conclusions, try to identify the author's intended audience. The *audience* includes the people the author hopes to reach with her message. In general, authors have in mind particular audience members who share qualities, such as similar backgrounds, characteristics, experiences, assumptions, and values.

Whereas sometimes it is obvious who the audience is, usually the reader must find out who the intended audience might be by using inference skills. As an example, read the paragraph below:

> The past several years have seen a marked decline in college placement scores in reading and math. Whereas in 2001, approximately 35 percent of college freshmen tested into developmental reading and math courses; in 2011, the number was closer to 50 percent. This climbing statistic has several ramifications. Colleges need to be prepared for an influx of students who cannot be placed into college-level classes until they do the requisite developmental series. They must increase the number of sections they offer in reading and math, which could mean hiring more professors who specialize in developmental curriculum. Taking a serious look at the nation's high school programs in these areas is also a primary concern.

At first glance you might think this paragraph is addressed to college students, but that is not the case. A closer look allows you to infer its audience. Words like "ramifications" and "influx" suggest an educated audience. "Developmental curriculum" and "requisite developmental series" are considered jargon of higher education. Finally, the suggestion to investigate what is happening in high school reading and math programs should give you a clue that the passage is directed to professionals in the field of education, specifically college administrators, counselors, and professors.

Use the following strategies to find out about an author's intended audience:

- **Locate the source.** Find out all you can about the source of the material. Typical sources are textbooks, newspapers, magazines, professional journals, books, and pamphlets.
- **Acknowledge the occasion.** See if the material was published in response to a specific event. For example, did an author write an impassioned plea for volunteers after a natural disaster? Did the author publish a reaction to a controversial sociology experiment conducted recently in the field?
- **Check level.** Oftentimes you can learn a lot about the intended audience by noticing how challenging, or easy, the vocabulary, concepts, and sentence structures are. Technical jargon suggests that the author is targeting professionals who are educated and experienced in the field, for instance. Annotating the text should give you clues about the author's intended audience based on the author's word choices and style.
- **Examine audience characteristics.** Try to find out what audience members have in common, such as profession, political ideology, religious affiliation, nationality, and so on. How might these characteristics influence their attitudes, needs, and values?
- **Research other works by the author.** On a bookseller's website, on an author's home page, or in your college library, look up other works published by the author and see if you can find additional hints about the audience.

FOR FURTHER STUDY

1. Read an article or book that is assigned for another class. Research likely audience members. Write a paragraph that describes the author's intended audience.
2. Write a short essay explaining how the character trait of intellectual curiosity assists you as you conduct additional research that may lead you to better inferences.

Inferring an author's purpose

Purpose is the reason or goal an author has for writing a text. Writers have a point they hope to make in reaching out to an audience. As with determining the author's audience, the reader must use inference skills in order to infer what the author's purpose might be. The three basic purposes are *to inform, to persuade*, or *to entertain*. However, usually authors have more specific, focused goals in mind:

- Authors who write *to inform* may want to explain, introduce, provide background information, give directions, or define.
- Authors who write *to persuade* may want to convince, suggest, argue, express an opinion, or sell something.
- Authors who write *to entertain* may want to be funny, inspiring, touching, scary, shocking, exciting, or emotional.

Taking note of audience, word choices, and context can help you infer an author's purpose. For example, if a writer uses convincing word choices in an advertisement, which causes the intended audience to desire and purchase a product, then it is likely that the purpose is to persuade (specifically, to sell something). The following examples should help you recognize purpose in other texts you are assigned to read:

To inform

Honey, a sweet food made by bees, comes from nectar. Honeybees take nectar from flowers, store it in beehives, and then the excess is collected by beekeepers to be processed and sold to consumers. The bee colony depends on honey as a food and energy source when food is scarce. In a typical hive, there is one queen bee and many male drone bees (for fertilization) and female worker bees. If properly handled, stored, and sealed, honey will not spoil for years. People use honey as a sweetener in tea, baked goods, and as a spread for bread and biscuits.

To persuade

You should make exercise a regular part of your routine. If you make it a habit, like brushing your teeth or reading the newspaper, then you will not let other things get in the way of your daily exercise. Obviously, exercise improves your appearance. If you are hanging on to some extra pounds, then you can reach your ideal, healthy weight by eating right and exercising regularly. Even if you are already at your target weight, exercise will tone your muscles and give your skin a healthy glow. Exercise has been proven to increase good health and longevity. In addition, exercise improves mood and mental processes. On top of all of this, exercise can be fun! Get some friends together to walk, run, play basketball, or take a dance class. You can fit in exercise easily throughout your day—take the stairs instead of the elevator, and bike to work instead of driving a few miles. Given all of these benefits, the time you devote to exercise is perhaps the most important part of the day.

To entertain

Are my friends *really* the people they appear to be on Facebook? The people I thought I knew so well—former classmates, coworkers, relatives—cannot possibly be as obnoxious as they seem on their Facebook profiles. Let's look at Lou, for an example: mild-mannered accountant by day, embarrassingly vain bodybuilder at night. Lou posts photos of his biceps, triceps, abs, but, thankfully, stops short of his glutes. His photos pale in comparison to Miranda's photos of herself in a variety of drinking establishments. Oh look! There's Miranda drinking a martini!

Now she's drinking a gin and tonic! I will say, however, at least I get to *see* Lou and Miranda in their photos: Kasey only posts pictures of her children; Felix only posts pictures of his parakeet; and Drake only posts pictures of food he is about to consume. As if the photos aren't bad enough, then there are the status updates that tell me more about my friends than I ever wanted to know. I am intimately acquainted with Milt's marital misfortunes, Pat's political pet peeves, and Rhonda's religious rants. After a few minutes on Facebook, I realize I prefer my friends the old-fashioned way—face-to-face, where they were too polite to overshare.

The following tips can help you determine the author's purpose:

1. **Annotate**. Circle, underline, or highlight any word choices, details, or hints that indicate the author's purpose.
2. **Look at the details**. Details can tell you a lot about the author's purpose. Writers who want *to inform* will rely on facts, statistics, expert testimony, and objective information. Those authors who wish *to persuade* readers will use opinions and words with strong connotations. When authors focus on creative and interesting details, they are trying *to entertain*.
3. **Consider the source**. Certain sources are almost always written with one main purpose in mind. For example, newspapers, textbooks, and professional journal articles tend to be informative. Political campaign literature and retailer advertising copy are typically persuasive. Finally, best-selling novels and popular magazines about celebrity gossip are entertaining.
4. **See the forward or preface**. If the source contains a forward or preface, read it to see if the author directly tells readers what her purpose is.
5. **Consider connotations**. Remember to annotate and examine word choices for strong connotations. Words that make a recommendation (like *should* and *ought to*) tend to suggest a persuasive purpose.

6. **Stay open-minded and flexible.** Sometimes authors have more than one purpose in mind, and you might have to change your initial reaction if new information becomes available. Also, purposes may overlap; it is entirely possible for an author to write an entertaining piece that also informs or persuades.

FOR FURTHER STUDY

1. Go to your college library and locate a source for each of the three purposes: to inform, to persuade, and to entertain.
2. Read a book, passage, or article assigned for another class. Identify the author's primary purpose. Then, identify the author's more specific purpose (for example, an author who writes to entertain may have the more specific purpose in mind of being funny).

Inferring word connotation

Throughout this chapter, we have been telling you to pay attention to word choice. The connotations of the author's words tell you much about the author's opinion about the topic. *Denotation* means the dictionary definition of a word; *connotation* refers to the feelings associated with the word. Some connotations elicit emotions that are strong enough to create *images* (mental pictures) in the audience members' minds. An example is the word "honor." While the denotative meaning explains that honor is a person's integrity or morality, the connotation associated with honor might include such moving images as a soldier returning to a battlefield despite being injured, or a witness telling the truth in court despite being wrenched by the testimony.

Skilled writers will purposefully use words that provoke certain emotions in their readers, both positive and negative. As you annotate, notice those emotive words—words that have particular emotions associated with them. A thesaurus or dictionary will provide you with synonyms, so you can get a sense of how changing the word to one of its synonyms might affect the overall feeling of the passage (as a bonus, this is a good way to boost your vocabulary). You can infer what the author wants readers to feel or picture given specific, deliberate word choices. Use the following steps for inferring when a word has strong connotations:

1. **Refer to a dictionary.** Make sure you know the word's denotative definition first.
2. **Consider context.** Look at the other words and ideas surrounding the word (context) to see what they suggest about the word's connotation. A word having a negative connotation in one context might have a positive one in another context.
3. **Check the thesaurus.** Think about how changing the word to a synonym might change the connotation.
4. **Annotate any images.** When you annotate, circle words that elicit strong images and jot down your mental picture in the margin.

FOR FURTHER STUDY

1. Reread the sample *purpose* paragraphs (to inform, to persuade, and to entertain) on pages 39–41. Circle any words that have strong connotations. Do you get an overall positive or negative feeling?
2. Read an article or book that is assigned for another class. Annotate carefully for words that have strong connotations. Jot down the images in the margin. Overall, are the author's word choices suggesting positive or negative emotions? Explain why you think the author selected specific words.

Inferring an author's tone

Readers can infer an author's tone much like they can infer audience, purpose, and connotations. *Tone* is the author's voice—the attitude or feeling expressed through the text. Tone is suggested by subject matter, word choice (connotations), sentence structure, and punctuation.

Authors take into account both audience and purpose when choosing a particular tone to express. For example, if an author is writing to persuade an audience of college freshmen to research potential careers, then a bossy or overbearing tone will not be as effective as a helpful and informative tone.

When you are face-to-face, it is fairly easy to infer a friend's mood or tone through his voice, facial expressions, word choices, and body language. Since you do not have the benefit of face-to-face interaction with an author, you have to depend on other information, such as word choices, sentence structure, and the context of the reading. Practically any adjective you could use to describe someone's personality could be used to describe an author's tone. The following is just a partial list of all the possible tones an author might express:

Academic	Condescending	Ironic
Angry	Effervescent	Persuasive
Argumentative	Formal	Sarcastic
Bewildered	Funny	Sentimental
Calm	Furious	Serious
Cheerful	Informative	Sincere
Concerned	Inspiring	Troubled

To infer an author's tone, do the following:

- **Read the text out loud.** You may be able to hear the author's voice or emotion if you say her words out loud.
- **Notice sentence structure and punctuation.** Sometimes, short sentences suggest anger, impatience, or excitement. Complex sentences might suggest an academic or serious tone. All-caps or exclamation points can convey powerful emotions (both positive and negative).
- **Think about audience.** Remember, of course, that authors want their audience to keep reading and to be informed, persuaded, or entertained. Infer how the author's tone would affect likely readers.
- **Consider the author's purpose.** What tone would best accomplish the author's purpose? If the author uses a tone that doesn't seem to fit his purpose, try to figure out why.

— FOR FURTHER STUDY —

1. Look up any of the tone words above that are unfamiliar to you.
2. Brainstorm a list of additional tone words, thinking of adjectives you would use to describe people.
3. Reread the sample *purpose* paragraphs (to inform, to persuade, and to entertain) on pages 39–41. How would you describe the author's tone in each one?
4. Pretend you must write a letter to your landlord explaining why you are going to be late with your rent. Write three different versions using three different tones. Trade with a classmate and see if you can each determine the tones expressed. Then, given the purpose and audience, decide which letter is most effective.

Throughout this chapter you learned about making inferences, particularly about the author's audience, purpose, word connotations, and tone. Remember, of course, that an inference is a *reasonable* guess, so, at times, you will be making guesses that are incorrect. With practice, you will make better and better inferences.

Thinking about the author's audience, purpose, connotations, and tone help you to recognize that the author is a real person who has a desire to connect with readers through writing. As a reader, your job is to figure out both the stated and implied messages that the author wants to convey to you. The act of making inferences gets you closer to the author and closer to understanding the entire passage.

Learning More

1. Reread a few paragraphs from a book you enjoyed. Write a paragraph explaining the author's purpose, audience, connotations, and tone. Does analyzing the text carefully help you understand and enjoy the text more, or less? Write another paragraph that describes how identifying additional information affects your enjoyment of the text.

2. Explain how the character trait of trust in reason relates to drawing conclusions.

3. Describe an instance in which you made an inference that was incorrect. How did you find out that you were wrong? How did you incorporate new information in order to draw a more logical conclusion?

5

RECOGNIZING AND JUDGING ARGUMENTS

The next essential skill to master in your quest to become a critical reader and thinker is the ability to analyze and evaluate arguments. When you hear the word "argument," you might think of a disagreement—two people yelling at each other—but that's not the kind of argument we refer to in this chapter. An *argument* is a claim backed up by one or more reasons offered in its support. The *claim* of the argument is the statement that the person making the argument wants you to accept as true. The reasons supporting the claim are known as *premises* or *evidence*.

It is crucial to learn to identify and judge arguments, because arguments are everywhere. Almost all written works that are not narratives (stories) make arguments in some form. If you are hesitant, your friend is likely to present an argument as to why she wants you to skip work and go to the movies with her. Commercials are presenting arguments when they try to persuade you to buy a product. Politicians make arguments to get you to vote for them. Different institutions and groups will present arguments about why you should believe a myriad of ideas. It should be clear then, that you need to be able to figure out when someone is making an argument and decide if that argument is convincing. Otherwise, you might spend your money or time on the wrong products, vote for an inferior candidate, or believe untrue claims.

Recognizing arguments

Even knowing what an argument is, it's not always easy to identify one. The key is to remember that reasons have to be presented in support of a claim—something the author declares to be true. As mentioned above, these reasons are referred to as premises or evidence; you may also think of these reasons as the *proof* of the argument. When the claim of the argument is supported by proof, and the claim is intended to follow logically from the proof, you have an argument.

If no proof is provided in support of a claim, all you have is an assertion; you don't have an argument. You might hear someone say:

"You should study hard in school."

All this person is doing is making an assertion, providing an unsupported opinion. The speaker needs to provide evidence to support this opinion if he wants to convince you. Without evidence, he hasn't made an argument. But he *has* made an argument if he says:

"You should study hard in school, because then you will be able to get the job you want."

The statement "you should study hard in school" is the claim or conclusion of the argument, and the statement "you will be able to get the job you want" is the evidence or proof. Of course, more than one piece of evidence can be provided in support of a conclusion. The statements that make up an argument also need to be able to be proven true or false. Poetic statements, questions, and exclamations can't be proven true or false, so they can't serve as the evidence or conclusion in an argument.

Sometimes cue words will provide hints that an author is making an argument. If an author uses words like *thus, therefore, so,* or *consequently,* you might expect to find a conclusion to an argument. If an author uses words like *because, for example,* or *the reasons are,* you might expect to find evidence being offered in support of a conclusion. You have to be attentive, though, because sometimes these words won't be present when an argument is being made, and sometimes they will be present when an argument has not been made. You should consider these words a suggestion to look more closely at what you are reading to figure out if an argument is being made.

Sometimes your best clue that someone is making an argument is the context or the situation in which it is being presented. For example, if you are reading an article criticizing Twitter, you might see the following paragraph:

> Twitter seems to be making people stupider. Tweets essentially consist of sound bites, mini-thoughts of 140 or fewer words. People who use Twitter on a regular basis are training their brains to think in a condensed way. They are learning to be shallow thinkers. People should not use Twitter.

You won't find any of the cue words in the paragraph above, yet you should easily be able to tell that the author is presenting an argument. The fact that the text is being critical of Twitter should help you see that the last sentence of the passage is a conclusion, which is supported by the reasons given earlier in the passage.

Evidence

Recognizing evidence

As we discussed, evidence, or proof, consists of the statements that provide support for a conclusion. For something to count as evidence, you must be able to prove it true or false. For example, "Joseph was in El Paso the night of the twenty-fifth" could be declared true or false: Either he was there or he wasn't. But a statement like "GE brings good things to life" is just a poetic expression that sounds good but doesn't actually mean anything specific; you can't really say it is true or false. Many poetic statements, such as metaphors, can't be proven true or false, and therefore aren't evidence.

Evidence must be presented in the form of a statement. It can't be an exclamation, a command, or a question (unless it's a rhetorical question, meaning a question that has an obvious answer). Consider the following two arguments:

> Alien life exists, because probability dictates that with all the Earth-like planets that exist, some must have evolved life.

> Alien life exists. I know it, because I saw an extraterrestrial.

Both offer reasons to believe that alien life exists, so they count as evidence. Whether they are convincing arguments has to be evaluated—we will get to that next.

Evidence cannot be an explanation of how a belief was acquired, nor can it be an affirmation of belief (a statement of how much the person believes the conclusion). Imagine that instead of the argument about alien life given above, an author stated:

> Aliens exist. I know it, because I was raised to believe in them.

Even though you see the cue word *because,* the statement doesn't actually contain any evidence, because it doesn't provide real support for the claim. It doesn't give someone else reason to believe that aliens exist; it's just an explanation of how the author acquired the belief. The author hasn't provided any proof that aliens do exist. Similarly, if she had said, "I know aliens exist, because I really, really believe in them," she wouldn't be doing any better. She would simply be affirming her belief (telling you how strong her belief is). So to summarize, when trying to figure out if a statement can serve as the evidence of an argument, do the following:

- **Look for reasons offered in support of a claim.** Make sure the reasons provide proof for the claim.
- **Ignore commands, exclamations, and questions.** They can't be evidence, because they aren't true or false.
- **Make sure the statement can be proven true or false.** If you can't assign it a truth-value or if it's a poetic statement, it's not support for a conclusion.
- **If the author simply states how he acquired the belief, or how much he believes the belief or wants it to be true, it's not evidence.** Such statements don't prove anything.

Practice

Directions: Examine the following statements. Identify which ones make arguments by underlining all the statements that could serve as evidence, and double-underling statements that follow from the evidence and serve as conclusions. Write an *A* in each blank if the statement makes an argument. Write an *N* if it does not.

_____ 1. Since you practiced your ballet every day, you should do well in your recital.

_____ 2. Man, ghosts are so cool. I really hope they exist.

_____ 3. All of the galaxies are traveling away from each other, and the universe is filled with background microwave radiation. The current state of the universe is the result of a Big Bang.

_____ 4. Make sure you give me back the Blu-ray you borrowed. I promised I'd lend it to my friend Bob, who really enjoys comedies.

_____ 5. Exercising three or more times per week is beneficial. This is clear because multiple credible studies showed that people who did so lowered their blood pressure, lost weight, and had less bad cholesterol.

Evaluating evidence

Recognizing evidence is important, but the main point of picking out the evidence is to see if it is good or not. The critical thinker's attitude of skepticism will serve you well when evaluating evidence—remember not to accept a statement just because you are told it's true or because someone wrote it down. Check it for yourself.

When you evaluate evidence, you consider the following:

- Is it relevant?
- Is it sufficient?
- Is it made up primarily of facts, opinions, or reasoned judgments?
- Is it accurate?

Evidence should be *relevant* to the conclusion—it should closely and directly relate to it. If evidence is *irrelevant*, it's unrelated and unimportant. Sometimes authors will introduce irrelevant evidence, either deliberately or accidentally, because they are unsure about what constitutes solid, relevant evidence. Here is an example of an argument that employs irrelevant evidence:

> Pit bulls bite hundreds of people every year. Pit bulls can be dangerous around children, and they also were bred for the

sole purpose of fighting. For these reasons, it is clear that people should be required to have permits for their pets.

The conclusion—that people should be required to have permits for their pets—has very little to do with pit bulls, since "pets" includes cats, fish, hamsters, and lizards. The evidence doesn't relate to the conclusion. Another thing to take into account when checking relevance is to see if any relevant information has been purposely left out. Has the author omitted information that might weaken his case?

The next factor to take into consideration is *sufficiency*, meaning has the author included enough evidence to adequately support the conclusion. The amount of evidence needed depends on how extraordinary or far-reaching the claim of the argument is. If the conclusion is an everyday statement, such as the claim that one candy bar contains more calories than a different candy bar, then the only evidence needed might be the nutritional information on their labels. But if the conclusion is that a living dinosaur exists in South America, far more evidence—such as pictures, spores, eggs, DNA, and probably a carcass—would be necessary before you would accept such a claim.

The third factor is whether the evidence is fact, opinion, or reasoned judgment. A *fact* is a statement that can be objectively verified, meaning that anyone, regardless of his or her personal feelings or biases, can research and determine it to be true. Here is an example of a fact:

> The distance from the Earth to the Moon varies from 356,400 km to 406,700 km.

Facts make good evidence in arguments, and, as long as you verify that they are true, can generally be accepted.

An *opinion* is someone's personal judgment about a subject. Opinions are often matters of taste or bias, and they should generally be discounted as evidence. They do not offer strong support for most conclusions. Here is an example of an opinion:

> Rock music is better than country music.

This is clearly a matter of taste; you can't prove it true or false, and it would not serve as good evidence supporting a conclusion that your school should fund the study of rock music but should not fund the study of country music.

Reasoned judgment, also called *informed opinion*, is a special kind of opinion resulting from the research and experience of an expert in the field. You might also hear this type of opinion referred to as *expert testimony*. When you evaluate evidence, reasoned judgment should carry more weight than simple opinion. That's because such informed opinions are often necessary to help us understand what facts mean. For example, when the swine flu broke out in the United States in 2009, people rightfully turned to the Centers for Disease Control and Prevention (CDC) for reasoned judgment about how the disease would impact the country and what the mortality rate might be. It should be pretty obvious why you should consult the CDC's informed opinion on these matters before you ask your roommate, who works as a teller at a bank.

Lastly, you will need to check whether evidence is *accurate*. In other words, you'll have to find out if it is correct or not. You might be surprised at how many things you are commonly told are actually false. For example, you might have heard that humans only use 10 percent of their brains, or that eating turkey makes you sleepy. Both of these common "facts" are untrue. To check accuracy, you need to do two things: (1) Research the statements made. Look them up in reference sources or in books written by experts in the field. Do the sources you trust match the statements that make up the evidence you're evaluating? (2) Consider the source of the evidence.

Source credibility

Many times, the quality of the evidence depends on the quality of the source that provides the evidence. Biased sources that have agendas often issue evidence that is not trustworthy and that should not be credited. Evaluating sources is tricky, but very important. You will need to know how to evaluate print and online sources and how to evaluate authors themselves.

Evaluating print and online sources

Just because a statement has been printed in a book, magazine, newspaper, or online does not automatically mean that it is trustworthy. You have to take the following considerations into account when evaluating printed and online sources:

- Does the source contain a bibliography, in-text citations, a table of contents, and an index?
- Is the source current? The more recent the date of publication, the better. This is especially important in technical and scientific fields.
- Has the source been peer-reviewed? Peer review is a process wherein acknowledged experts in the field check to see that the publication is credible. Peer review dramatically increases trustworthiness. Also look to see if the work has been edited: Editors check a work for clarity and grammatical errors, and they can also make recommendations about content.
- Is the publisher reputable? Many publishing houses or companies have agendas—they are out to advance a specific political, religious, or ideological cause. These tend to be less credible publishers. As a rule of thumb, sources published by professional organizations or university presses are reputable.
- Especially if the work has been published online, can you easily identify the responsible party and contact that person if necessary? Having to answer for what they publish tends to force authors to be more credible.

To evaluate an author, you should consider the following issues:

- Does the author seem knowledgeable about the subject? Does the author have a degree in the field that he or she writes about? Does the author have experience working in the field? Do other professionals in the field regard the author as credible? What is his or her reputation in the field?
- Why did the author write the text? Remember what you learned about authorial purpose in chapter 4: Is the author trying to inform, persuade, or entertain you? Does the author have a personal or ideological reason for wanting you to accept his or her argument?
- Does the author seem biased? We will discuss more about bias in chapter 6, but, in short, *bias* is an unfair judgment.

Often insults or strong, *loaded language*—language that is intended to affect your emotions in a powerful way—are indications that an author is biased. If he or she calls the other side names or labels contradictory arguments as "horrible" or "stupid," you can safely consider that author biased. A biased author will not be fair-minded and will often give evidence that is not relevant, that is insufficient, that is mere opinion, or that is inaccurate.

FOR FURTHER STUDY

1. Write a one-page essay in which you consider why open-mindedness, skepticism, and fair-mindedness are especially important when evaluating evidence and source credibility.
2. Find an argument in one of the readings you have to do for homework or in an outside reading. Identify the evidence and evaluate it. Is the source credible? Explain your findings.

Logic

After you have identified and examined the evidence in an argument, you have to make sure that the logic of the argument is compelling. The logic of the argument is the reasoning that links the evidence to the conclusion and allows you to infer the conclusion from the evidence. If the logic of the argument is faulty, even if the evidence is good, the argument fails.

Deductive logic

There are two main types of logic: deductive logic and inductive logic. *Deductive logic* is logic that guarantees that a conclusion follows from its premises. Usually, a deductive argument begins with a generalization and draws a specific conclusion from it. Consider the following argument:

> Anyone who turns in a library book late for any reason must pay a fine. Samson turned in a late library book, so he owes money to the library.

This is a deductive argument. It starts with a generalization: "Anyone who turns in a library book late for any reason must pay a fine," and the argument draws a specific conclusion from the generalization. There is no way that the conclusion could be false if the evidence (in this case, the first two statements in the argument) is true. Samson definitely owes a fine.

So, to see if an argument is deductive, determine if the premises are more general than the conclusion and if the specific conclusion is intended to follow with certainty. Once you have determined that an argument is deductive and found that the evidence is true, you can check to see if there is any way whatsoever the conclusion could be false. If the conclusion has to be true, the deductive argument uses good logic. Here is an example of a deductive argument that uses bad logic:

All dogs need to eat. Zoey needs to eat, so Zoey is a dog.

If you assume that the evidence ("all dogs need to eat" and "Zoey needs to eat") is true, is there any way you can think of that Zoey wouldn't be a dog? Well, of course Zoey could be a cat, a parakeet, or a human being. The logic of this argument is bad.

FOR FURTHER STUDY
---

1. Go online to the OWL at Purdue (http://owl.english.purdue .edu/) to learn more about deductive arguments. Write a short paragraph that explains what you learned.
2. Research syllogisms. Define them and relate them to deductive arguments.

Inductive logic

Inductive logic is logic that examines specific instances and draws a general conclusion from them. For that reason, the premises of an inductive argument are more specific than the conclusion. The conclusion of an inductive argument is never guaranteed, whereas the conclusion of a logical deductive argument is 100 percent guaranteed. Consider the following argument:

> Studies show that of 1,000 people who smoked cigarettes, lung cancer occurred at a far higher rate than among a similar population of nonsmokers. Smoking causes cancer.

The evidence in this argument is specific—1,000 people whom you could look up and talk to if you so desired. The conclusion is a generalization, and an uncertain one at that. While the argument strongly suggests that smoking causes cancer, it can't ever prove it 100 percent. With evidence like this staring you in the face, however, you would be foolish to discount the conclusion.

So, to recognize an argument as inductive, look to see if the premises are more specific than the conclusion, which will likely be a generalization. Then check to make sure that the conclusion is strongly suggested by the evidence. Make sure that the conclusion is probable.

It may help you to understand that deductive logic and inductive logic are closely connected. The generalizations that serve as the major premise in a deductive argument were acquired by careful inductive reasoning. The example below should help to illustrate this point:

Inductive Logic	Deductive Logic
Evidence: In a recent survey of 1,200 people, employees in helping professions (such as teaching and nursing) report higher job satisfaction than those employees in careers that pay better but that have less contact with people (such as accounting and engineering).	Generalization: **Careers in fields that encourage you to help others are very satisfying.**
Evidence: I have spoken with a lot of teachers and nurses who report the same attitude as reported in the survey.	Evidence: Walter has chosen a career in social work.
Conclusion: **Careers in fields that encourage you to help others are very satisfying.**	Specific conclusion: **Walter will find his career to be satisfying.**

Fallacies of induction

One thing that often makes an inductive argument faulty is that it commits a *logical fallacy* (a mistake in reason or logic that leads to a conclusion that seems plausible, but which is not properly entailed by the evidence). Many types of fallacies exist, and you would need to study extensively to learn them all, but here are some of the most common ones:

- **Ad hominem:** Attacking the person rather than the argument. "How can Congressman Smith be right about the budget? He is working on his fourth marriage!" is an example.
- **Appeal to the masses:** Arguing that something is true because lots of people believe it. "You know ghosts exist. Millions of people believe in them," is an example.
- **Begging the question:** The conclusion is simply a restatement of the premise. "The death penalty is morally impermissible because capital punishment is wrong," is an example.
- **Either-or:** The arguer artificially narrows the field of choices down to just two, when, in reality, more exist. "Either we raise school taxes, or we cut music, gym, and art," is an example.
- **False authority:** Relying on the testimony of a nonexpert in the field. "Stephen Hawking believes that Keynesian economics is the correct way to balance the budget," is an example. Stephen Hawking is a physicist, not an economist.
- **False cause:** A cause is misidentified. Often it involves assuming that because two things happened together or in quick succession, one caused the other. "I broke a mirror, and then I had bad luck. Breaking mirrors is bad luck," is an example.
- **Hasty generalization:** Drawing a conclusion from insufficient evidence. "I took echinacea, and my cold went away. Echinacea cures colds," is an example. Just because it happened once is no proof that it cures colds.
- **Red herring:** Using irrelevant, distracting evidence to support a conclusion. "Reporting the crime is the ethical thing to do, but think of the embarrassment it would cause you and our company. It should not be reported," is an example. Embarrassment is irrelevant.

- **Slippery slope:** An arguer suggests that taking an action will inevitably give rise to a chain of events that will lead to undesirable consequences. "If we raise taxes, all of our businesses will flee overseas and we will all be destitute," is an example.
- **Straw man:** Misrepresenting an argument in order to make it easier to refute. "You believe that we should cut national defense? Why do you want our country to lose wars?," is an example.

If you find these fallacies in an inductive argument, the conclusion could still be true, or it could be false, but you know the argument is bad and should be rejected.

While recognizing and evaluating arguments is an extremely important part of being a critical reader, it is also tricky and difficult. The attitudes of a critical thinker, especially skepticism, fair-mindedness, and persistence, will help you as you work to master this skill, and the payoff is immense. If you can evaluate arguments, you will be one step closer to being able to discern what is true. In fact, you may find it exciting to pinpoint weaknesses in whatever arguments are presented to you, and, with practice, you will become an expert at scrutinizing arguments for truth and logic.

Learning More

1. Revisit the argument you found in the activity on page 55. Now that you have evaluated it for author and source credibility, identify which kind of logic the argument uses and check to see if the logic is good. If it is deductive, is the conclusion guaranteed by the premises? If it is inductive, is the conclusion strongly suggested and does the argument avoid fallacies?
2. Using the Internet or your library, look up and define more inductive fallacies. Try to invent examples of your own.
3. Why might it be difficult to be fair-minded when evaluating arguments? Explain in detail. Have you ever caught yourself being unfair when considering someone else's argument?

6

DEALING WITH
WORLDVIEWS AND BIAS

The last skill you need to acquire is *monitoring*. You must be able to examine yourself and others to see if worldviews and biases are getting in the way of fair, rational judgments. Worldviews and biases are the result of how you were raised, what events and challenges you experienced in your past, and what communities and viewpoints you associate yourself with. Everyone has them. It is necessary, though, to recognize your own worldviews and biases so that they don't cause you to be unfair or to make bad decisions.

Worldviews

A *worldview* is a framework of beliefs and values by which you understand the world and navigate your way through it. Essentially, a worldview is what you use to make sense of the world and your place in it. Your worldview helps you answer the following questions:

- What is true about the world?
- How did the world get here?
- How did I get here?
- What matters most in life?
- What should I strive to do or be?
- How do I attain my goals?

Everyone has a worldview; it would be impossible to avoid them. Having a worldview can be positive; it can help make the world less confusing and frightening. Furthermore, it can provide a sense of connection with others who share your beliefs.

So what is the problem with worldviews? After all, everyone is a product of culture and background. The problem is not so much that worldviews are the lens through which we make sense of our world, but that worldviews often remain unexamined. We should base our judgments on critical thinking and objective reasoning. However, if we never become aware of our worldview and never critically examine it, we will tend to make decisions based on what we assume to be true, rather than what the evidence suggests. This is because every worldview contains certain blind spots, weaknesses, and biases. The world is so contradictory and complex that no single worldview can account for it.

Another problem with worldviews is that they can cause us to become ethnocentric, which means believing that our ethnicity is superior to other ethnicities. They can also make us think that our particular influences, such as our religion, family traditions, and politics, are better than the other options available in the world. Recognizing this tendency can make you more sensitive to other people who have different backgrounds, ethnicities, traditions, and politics; it will help you get along better with people who have different worldviews.

Being tolerant of differing worldviews is extremely important, since people decide what matters and how they should behave based on their own worldviews, and, unfortunately, conflicting worldviews lead to strife. When worldviews are different enough, they can lead to conflicts that are often nearly irresolvable. For example, the worldviews of some fundamentalist Muslims—that Islam should be the official religion of a state, that Islam is destined to be the dominant religion in the world, and that extreme means of conversion are warranted—is incompatible with the worldviews of many Westerners, who believe that the state should not espouse a religion, that people should be free to choose their own religion, and that extreme means of conversion are never warranted. This clash of worldviews explains a great deal about the conflicts the United States, Europe, and the Middle East have engaged in during the twenty-first century.

For this reason, it is crucial that every critical thinker make an effort to become aware of his or her worldview and strive to be more tolerant and understanding of the worldviews of others.

Practice

Directions: On another sheet of paper, explore the following questions so that you can better understand your own worldview.

1. How was the universe created?
2. Are human beings special, or are they simply another species of animal?
3. If you could choose any country or culture to live in, which would it be and why?
4. What, if any, is the correct religion? Why?
5. If you could choose any profession and be guaranteed to be successful in it, what would you choose? What do you think this says about your values?
6. What is the worst thing a human being could possibly do? Why?

FOR FURTHER STUDY

1. Examine your own worldview. Why do you believe what you believe? Did you arrive at your beliefs using reason, logic, and evidence, or do you hold your beliefs because you were told they were true, or because you were raised to believe in them?
2. Choose a worldview that is radically different from your own. Research the worldview you chose. How do you think someone who holds that worldview would answer the questions above?

Identifying worldviews as you read

While reading critically, identifying an author's worldview will allow you to uncover the author's assumptions. *Assumptions* are beliefs one takes for granted as being true. An assumption is something an author doesn't give an explanation for—it's just assumed the to be the case (that's why it's called an *assumption*). Many times, assumptions are comprehensive statements that ground an author's viewpoint. For instance, we all tend to share certain basic assumptions—that other people exist and generally have similar thought processes to our own, that gravity will continue to function as it has always done in the past, that the outside world actually exists, and so on. But authors also have more precise assumptions that come from their worldviews. For example, an author who is politically conservative might hold the basic assumption that if one works hard, he can raise his status in life; that everyone has roughly equal chances; and that regulations will have a chilling effect on businesses. But an author with a liberal political outlook might assume that hard work alone is often not enough to bring success; that some people are born into situations that give them unfair disadvantages in life; and that without regulations, businesses will often engage in unethical practices that leave consumers worse off. Starting from these opposing assumptions, both authors are likely to analyze the same evidence differently and draw different conclusions from it.

Recognizing an author's worldview, then, will give you an insight into why the author draws the inferences and conclusions he does. It will allow you to make sense of an argument that might otherwise totally confuse you. And it will also allow you to feel some tolerance and empathy for an author whose viewpoint is different from your own.

FOR FURTHER STUDY

1. Choose one of the reading assignments you have to do for homework. Do a short Internet search to learn about the author. Identify the likely worldview of the author. What assumptions does that worldview cause the author to make? How do those assumptions affect the author's point of view?

Bias

Worldviews can often lead to bias. *Bias* refers to an unfair or partial judgment held at the expense of other equally valid perspectives. When you are biased, you don't fairly judge an issue; instead, you allow your preconceived judgments to affect how you view it. Bias often leads to *prejudice*, an unjust opinion about a person or group of people, usually based on race, sex, age, social class, or other superficial outward characteristics. Biases feed into prejudices, because when you are biased, you are unable to see the commendable traits of the people you are prejudiced against. You are literally blind to their good sides, so your prejudice is affirmed.

Like your worldview, it is important that you recognize your biases and prejudices so that you can work on not allowing them to affect your judgments and decisions. The character trait of fair-mindedness is especially important when it comes to bias: If you are fair-minded, you will be less biased.

Practice

Directions: Read the following statements and note whether you agree or disagree with them.

1. Capital punishment is wrong.
2. Abortion should be legal.
3. Marriage should only be permissible between a man and a woman.
4. Women are more sensitive and emotional, while men are more tough and straightforward.
5. Certain races and ethnicities are better at certain sports.
6. Poor people are lazy.
7. Rich people are greedy.
8. Rock stars are drug addicts.
9. Athletes are not generally smart.
10. My country is the best country in the world.

After you have taken note of your gut reactions to each of the statements, consider your responses and try to understand why you responded the way you did. Can you support your responses with evidence and reasoned argument, or were your answers simply based on "the way things are"? If your responses are simply "natural," rather than the result of rational judgments based on facts and evidence, they are the result of biases or prejudices. Working to uncover your own biases is essential because, as the writer Benjamin Hayden said, "A bias recognized is a bias sterilized."

Identifying bias as you read

You have worked to uncover your own biases, but it is also very important to recognize when authors are biased. To recognize bias in a text, you need to examine the writing situation, as well as the language the author uses.

The writing situation

The *writing situation* refers to the circumstances that prompted an author to write, the author's background and biography, the author's purpose, and the author's audience. Recognizing these things will alert you to potential authorial bias. To determine the writing situation, ask yourself the following questions:

- **Who is the writer and what are his or her credentials?** Is he or she affiliated with a certain organization, profession, religion, political party, etc.? What is the author's professional background? Does the author have a degree or expertise in the subject that he or she is writing about?
- **What event happened to prompt the author to write?** What outside circumstance led the author to produce the text?
- **Where was the text published?** What do you know about the publisher? What is the publisher's reputation?
- **Who is the text intended for?** Who is the audience? What assumptions does the audience make? What worldview does the audience hold? Is the audience likely to already agree with the author's point of view?
- **What is the purpose of the piece?** What is the author hoping to have the audience believe or do?

By understanding the situation in which the author wrote, you should be able to say whether the author is potentially biased before you even read the text. For example, suppose you are assigned to read an article for a political science class. The article is concerned with the question of whether marijuana should be legalized. The author is a well-known marijuana legalization activist and an admitted marijuana user, and the article has been published on a website that is known for advocating legalization. Being aware of these facts about the writing situation, you should be on the lookout for bias. These facts ought to cause you to look more carefully and skeptically at what the author states. You should also know, though, that a biased author can still make a valid argument.

FOR FURTHER STUDY

1. Find a recent article that pertains to a controversial topic. Determine whether the author is potentially biased by figuring out the writing situation surrounding the article. Should you expect to find bias in the article or not? Explain your response.

Loaded language

The language an author chooses is a major clue as to whether or not the author is biased. Words that have a strong connotation, words that are insulting, and words that conjure strong emotions in the reader are clues that the writer is probably biased. Imagine that while reading an article, you came across the following passage:

> Lazy liberals in Congress want to continue their ridiculous policy of allowing even lazier Americans to suckle from the government welfare teat. This will cause honest, hard-working business owners to have to work even harder to support them.

Insults like "lazy" and "ridiculous," and animal images like "suckle from the government welfare teat" indicate that the author is biased against liberals and the poor, while words like "honest" and "hard-working" let you know that the author favors well-off business owners. These statements have no support apart from the impression created by the author's word choice. The writer is using her choice of words to influence readers to agree with her simply because of emotion and prejudice. In a case like this, when a writer uses language to attempt to persuade the reader without evidence or argumentation, the writer is using what is known as *loaded language*.

To check to see if an author uses loaded language, do the following:

- **Examine connotations.** Do the words create positive or negative feelings in you? What mental images do the words invoke?

- **Try out different word choices.** If the sentence was expressed differently, would your response change? Use a thesaurus to examine word choices more carefully. What other words could the author have chosen that would have changed the impression without changing the content of the message?

Practice

Directions: Read the following statements and identify the bias in each by underlining examples of loaded language.

1. Evil corporations want to strip the country of its precious natural resources.
2. You shouldn't give your hard-earned money to the lazy bums on the street.
3. Only smelly hippies joined the wacky animal rights movement.
4. Greedy politicians are always scheming to figure out a way they can maintain their death-grip on power.
5. Sneaky immigrants just want to creep into this country in order to steal the jobs from honest and legitimate American citizens.

FOR FURTHER STUDY

1. Revisit the article you chose for the exercise on the writing situation on page 66. Examine it for loaded language. Does the author choose words that have strong connotations or images? If so, what impression does the author intend to convey? Be specific.

Monitoring your own thinking so that you become aware of your worldviews and biases will allow you to be fair-minded while you evaluate what you read. Identifying the worldview and biases of an author will keep you from being manipulated. You will be less likely to be persuaded to accept the author's point of view for the wrong reason. That's why the ability to recognize worldviews and biases is such a crucial skill.

Learning More

1. Review various pieces of writing (for instance, blogs, magazines, newspapers) to find five examples of loaded language. Then bring these examples to class and present your findings.
2. Review the character traits of a critical thinker and reader. Besides fair-mindedness, could acquiring the other character traits provide some protection against being biased? Explain your reasoning.

7

READING AND THINKING FOR LIFE

By now, you have a basic understanding of the skills and character traits of a critical reader and thinker. You have learned that critical reading means thinking critically about what you're reading. In order to think critically, you need to become a good thinker, namely a person who has a certain cluster of character traits. Critical thinkers are curious, humble, open-minded, skeptical, fair-minded, and persistent. Critical thinkers have specific skills: They are able to comprehend, interpret, infer, analyze, monitor, and evaluate information and ideas. They apply these traits and skills to texts in order to understand what they are reading, recognize what is important in it, draw conclusions about it, and decide if it is believable. This is how a critical thinker becomes a critical reader.

In this text, you've learned about these traits and skills one at a time, so that you could easily understand them. When you read texts in the "real world," though, you won't use these skills in isolation. They are used together to complement each other, and when you examine a difficult text, you will need to use the skills and character traits all at once to read it critically. Your ability to comprehend will help you interpret and infer, which will help you analyze and evaluate, for example. Likewise, you won't just be humble or just curious; you will need to be humble, curious, skeptical, and so forth, all at the same time. By combining the traits and skills, you will be most successful.

The overview in this text, however, is only the first step. Becoming an expert critical reader and thinker is a process, and it can't be accomplished overnight. It is something you have to prioritize and practice. Similar to excelling in a sport or becoming proficient on a musical instrument, you have to dedicate yourself to it and practice it every chance you get. Just as you sometimes lose when you play a sport you are good at, you will sometimes struggle or even fail when you try to read and think critically. But if you keep trying and don't get discouraged, you will have the satisfaction of seeing your reading and thinking ability grow and become stronger than you ever thought it could be. You will become an excellent critical reader and thinker. By this point, we hope you'll agree that acquiring these reading and thinking skills is a worthwhile lifelong goal, one with many benefits. You've seen that critical reading and thinking can help you to achieve better grades in college, enjoy a rewarding job, and even manage life problems and travails. You will be more resilient, coming through difficult times in your life more easily. Reading and thinking well can unlock many doors and allow you to achieve your aspirations, goals, and dreams. Really, to an expert critical reader and thinker, the sky is the limit!

INDEX

ADDITIONAL TITLES IN THE **WESSKA**
(WHAT EVERY STUDENT SHOULD KNOW ABOUT...) SERIES:

- *What Every Student Should Know About Avoiding Plagiarism* (ISBN 0-321-44689-5)

- *What Every Student Should Know About Citing Sources with APA Documentation* (ISBN 0-205-49923-6)

- *What Every Student Should Know About Citing Sources with MLA Documentation* including 2009 MLA Guidelines (ISBN 0-205-11511-7)

- *What Every Student Should Know About Creating Portfolios* (ISBN 0-205-57250-2)

- *What Every Student Should Know About Listening* (ISBN 0-205-77807-0)

- *What Every Student Should Know About Practicing Peer Review* (ISBN 0-321-44848-0)

- *What Every Student Should Know About Preparing Effective Oral Presentations* (ISBN 0-205-50545-7)

- *What Every Student Should Know About Procrastination* (0-205-58211-7)

- *What Every Student Should Know About Reading and Studying the Social Sciences* (ISBN 0-137-14137-8)

- *What Every Student Should Know About Study Skills* (ISBN 0-321-44736-0)

- *What Every Student Should Know About Using a Handbook* (ISBN 0-205-56384-8)

- *What Every Student Should Know About Writing Across the Curriculum* (ISBN 0-205-58913-8)

- *What Every Student Should Know About World Literature* (ISBN 0-205-21166-6)

- *What Every Student Should Know About Writing About Literature* (ISBN 0-205-23655-3)

- *What Every Student Should Know About Learning English as a Second Language* (ISBN 0-205-23008-3)

- *What Every Student Should Know About Researching Online* (ISBN 0-205-85646-2)

- *What Every Student Should Know About Ten Common Errors* (ISBN 0-205-86546-1)